STEVE WYNN

Master of Opulence- betting big

Grant G. Greech

All rights reserved. No part of this publication may be reproduced, distributed, or transmitted in any form or by any means, including photocopying, recording, or other electronic or mechanical method, without the prior written permission of the publisher, except in the case of brief quotations embodied in critical reviews and certain other noncommercial uses permitted by the copyright law.

Copyright © Grant G. Greech, 2024.

TABLE OF CONTENTS

INTRODUCTION

CHAPTER 1: STEVE IS WHO?

Education and early upbringing

CHAPTER 2: HUMBLE BEGINNINGS

Entry into the Casino World

CHAPTER 3: REINVENTING LAS VEGAS

Revitalizing Downtown: The Golden Nugget's Transformation

The Mirage – The Game Changer

CHAPTER 4: BELLAGIO – THE PINNACLE OF LUXURY

Redefining Casino Culture: High-End Elegance in Las Vegas

CHAPTER 5: WYNN LAS VEGAS – A LEGACY BUILT IN GOLD

Wynn's International Expansion

CONCLUSION

INTRODUCTION

Steve Wynn is a name synonymous with transformation in the world of luxury resorts and gaming, but his influence goes far beyond the Las Vegas Strip. *Steve Wynn: Master of Opulence – Betting Big* delves deep into the life of a man who not only revolutionized the concept of a casino but also redefined what it means to experience luxury. From his early days, taking on his family's financial burdens after his father's death, to his rise as one of the most innovative figures in the hospitality industry, this book explores the risks, vision, and artistry that shaped his remarkable career.

Wynn's journey from the bingo parlors of the East Coast to the dazzling opulence of properties like The Mirage, Bellagio, and Wynn Las Vegas reveals a story of perseverance, creativity, and sheer boldness. His commitment to crafting experiences that exceed expectations set new standards in the industry, blending world-class entertainment, dining, and design into environments where guests were not just visitors, but part of an extraordinary narrative.

This book offers readers an inside look into how Wynn saw opportunities where others saw limitations—betting big on groundbreaking ideas that would transform Las Vegas into a global destination for luxury and leisure. It examines not only his business ventures but also the intricate details of his design philosophy, which marries art and architecture with high-stakes gaming. Through this lens, the book paints a portrait of a man who used opulence not just as a symbol of wealth but as a vehicle for unforgettable experiences.

Steve Wynn: Master of Opulence – Betting Big is more than a biography; it is a study of how one man's vision and relentless drive reshaped an entire industry, left an indelible mark on global hospitality, and set the stage for the luxury resorts of the future. Wynn's story is a testament to how big risks, bold creativity, and unwavering ambition can turn dreams into reality, even on the grandest scale.

CHAPTER 1: STEVE IS WHO?

Steve Wynn is a prominent American businessman and real estate developer, best known for his pivotal role in the transformation of Las Vegas into the luxury resort destination it is today. He played a key role in shaping the modern casino and hospitality industry, particularly through the creation and development of some of the most iconic resorts on the Las Vegas Strip.

Wynn first gained recognition as the CEO of Golden Nugget, where he helped transform the downtown Las Vegas property into a luxury destination. His reputation grew as he embarked on groundbreaking projects that would redefine luxury and entertainment in Las Vegas. Some of his most famous developments include The Mirage, which opened in 1989 and was the first luxury mega-resort on the Strip, followed by other notable properties such as Treasure Island, Bellagio, Wynn Las Vegas, and Encore. His developments introduced new levels of sophistication in design, dining, shopping, and entertainment, setting new standards in the hospitality industry.

In addition to his impact on Las Vegas, Wynn expanded his influence globally with projects in Macau, including Wynn Macau and Wynn Palace Cotai, where he introduced his signature brand of luxury to the burgeoning Asian market.

Wynn is also known for his passion for art, often integrating world-class art collections into his resorts, enhancing their aesthetic and cultural appeal. Over his career, he became synonymous with innovation in resort design, integrating experiences that go beyond gaming to create fully immersive luxury environments.

Though his career has been marred by controversy, including allegations of sexual misconduct that led to his resignation as CEO of Wynn Resorts in 2018, his contributions to the casino and hospitality industries remain significant. Wynn's vision and creativity played a crucial role in elevating Las Vegas from a gambling-centric destination to a world-renowned luxury resort city.

Education and early upbringing

Steve Wynn, born Stephen Alan Weinberg on January 27, 1942, in New Haven, Connecticut, was shaped by a combination of entrepreneurial spirit and the influence of his family's background. Wynn's upbringing provided a foundation that would later define his business acumen and leadership in the casino and luxury resort industry.

His father, Michael Weinberg, was a bingo parlor operator on the East Coast, and his mother, Zelma, was a homemaker. When Steve was just a child, the family changed their last name to "Wynn" to avoid the antisemitism prevalent in the U.S. during that time. Michael's work in the gambling business exposed Steve to the world of gaming from an early age, albeit on a much smaller scale than the grand casinos Steve would later build. Despite the modest success of his father's ventures, Michael struggled financially, which had a profound effect on Steve's perspective on money, risk, and opportunity.

Steve Wynn attended The Manlius School, a military prep school in upstate New York, where he developed a sense of discipline that would later serve him in his career. He then enrolled at the University of Pennsylvania, attending its prestigious Wharton School of Business. There, he studied English literature but was surrounded by the influence of finance and business, which would become central to his future endeavors. While at Wharton, Wynn honed his interest in leadership and entrepreneurial ventures. However, his education was abruptly interrupted when, at age 21, his father passed away due to heart complications, leaving Wynn with his family's significant gambling debts.

Wynn made the difficult decision to leave school and take responsibility for the family business, quickly immersing himself in the bingo parlors his father had operated. His ability to navigate the financial difficulties following his father's death showcased the resilience and determination that would become trademarks of his career. He successfully turned around the bingo parlors, which not only helped resolve his family's financial issues but also gave him valuable business experience.

Wynn's early exposure to gambling through his father's work, coupled with the discipline and focus he developed during his education, shaped his vision for larger opportunities in the casino and resort industry. This blend of family influence, entrepreneurial spirit, and formal education set the stage for Wynn's later groundbreaking contributions to the transformation of Las Vegas into a luxury destination, starting with his early investments in properties like the Golden Nugget and eventually leading to the development of iconic resorts like The Mirage, Bellagio, and Wynn Las Vegas.

Wynn's early years were marked by the responsibility of turning financial challenges into opportunity, a trait that carried throughout his career as he navigated the ups and downs of the gaming and hospitality industries. His early education and upbringing were crucial in shaping his business strategies, particularly his understanding of risk and his penchant for innovation in the luxury hospitality sector.

CHAPTER 2: HUMBLE BEGINNINGS

Steve Wynn's journey to becoming a transformative figure in the world of luxury resorts and casinos began in a much more modest setting. Born Stephen Alan Weinberg on January 27, 1942, in New Haven, Connecticut, Wynn's upbringing offered him an early exposure to the world of business, though not in the glitzy environments he would later create. His father, Michael Weinberg, was a bingo parlor operator, running small gambling operations that provided the family with a steady, though far from lavish, income. Wynn's early exposure to this world of chance and risk would shape his future in unexpected ways.

When Steve was a young boy, the family's last name was changed from Weinberg to Wynn, as his father sought to establish a more American-sounding identity, a move that reflected the aspirations and challenges of immigrant families in mid-century America. Despite these adjustments, the family's life was often financially precarious, with Wynn witnessing firsthand the instability that could accompany his father's ventures. This experience instilled in him both an understanding of risk and a desire for financial security and success.

Wynn's early education was shaped by both his family's financial struggles and their emphasis on hard work. He attended a prestigious private school, The Manlius School, in Syracuse, New York, where he excelled academically and became a respected leader among his peers. His years at Manlius imbued him with discipline, ambition, and a sense of drive that would fuel his future business endeavors. Wynn was an astute student, but his most significant lessons were those absorbed outside the classroom, watching his father navigate the turbulent world of bingo halls and low-stakes gambling.

In 1959, after completing high school, Wynn enrolled at the University of Pennsylvania, where he studied English literature. However, Wynn's focus soon shifted when, in

1963, just before his graduation, his father died unexpectedly during heart surgery, leaving the family in financial turmoil. At only 21, Wynn was faced with the daunting responsibility of managing his father's bingo business and supporting his mother, Zelma, and his younger brother, Kenneth. This period of his life marked a turning point, as he was thrust into the world of entrepreneurship far earlier than he had anticipated.

Taking over his father's modest bingo business, Wynn quickly demonstrated his business acumen, displaying a talent for organization, marketing, and understanding customer needs. Although he was operating on a small scale, Wynn's instincts for improvement and reinvention were already apparent. He revitalized the family business, but he also became aware that his ambitions extended far beyond the confines of bingo parlors. Wynn's drive to think bigger, take calculated risks, and embrace new opportunities began to crystalize during these years.

Wynn's time in the bingo business gave him a unique education in risk management and entrepreneurship, providing valuable lessons about the balance between daring ventures and cautious planning. The small stakes of the bingo world may have seemed a far cry from the multi-million-dollar projects he would later pursue, but these early years were critical in shaping Wynn's understanding of the business of gambling.

It was during this period that Wynn began seeking out new opportunities, eventually making his way west to Las Vegas, Nevada, where he would lay the foundations for his future empire. Las Vegas, with its burgeoning casino industry and growing reputation as an entertainment capital, attracted Wynn with its vast potential. His father's influence was never far from his thoughts, as he sought to apply the principles of gambling and risk he had learned in the bingo business to the world of high-stakes casinos.

Wynn's humble beginnings may have lacked the glamour and spectacle that would later define his career, but they were instrumental in shaping his perspective. From his father's bingo parlors to his early forays into entrepreneurship, these formative years taught Wynn the importance of seizing opportunities, managing risk, and cultivating a strong work ethic. These values would serve him well as he began his ascent in the casino and luxury resort industry, transforming not only his own fortunes but the landscape of Las Vegas itself. His humble beginnings became the bedrock upon which his legacy as a master of opulence was built.

Entry into the Casino World

Steve Wynn's entry into the casino world marked the beginning of a journey that would reshape Las Vegas and the global hospitality industry. After managing his father's bingo parlors following his untimely death, Wynn began searching for larger ventures, drawn to the possibilities that the rapidly growing casino business offered. His ambition and understanding of risk management, developed during his early entrepreneurial days, would serve as the foundation for his future success.

By the late 1960s, Wynn was determined to enter the high-stakes casino world. Las Vegas, which had already become a magnet for entertainment and gambling, was in the midst of a transformation. The city's glamour and allure attracted a wide range of entrepreneurs, but Wynn had something different in mind. Rather than simply replicating the casino models of the time, Wynn saw potential in offering guests an elevated experience, combining gambling with entertainment, luxury, and fine dining.

His first significant move into the casino industry came when he became involved with the Frontier Hotel, a famous property on the Las Vegas Strip. Wynn had developed a keen sense for real estate and business opportunities, and his early investment in the Frontier allowed him to gain invaluable experience and connections within the casino world. It was here that

Wynn's knack for recognizing potential in neglected or underdeveloped properties first became apparent.

One of Wynn's earliest and most pivotal business moves involved his acquisition of a small stake in the Frontier Hotel, a deal that allowed him to learn the inner workings of the casino business. This investment, though modest at the time, gave him access to the key players in Las Vegas, allowing him to build relationships with prominent casino operators and influential figures in the gaming industry. Wynn's entry into this world was not without its challenges, but his resilience and willingness to take calculated risks set him apart from others.

Wynn's first true foray into owning and operating a casino came with his purchase of the Golden Nugget, a then-downtown Las Vegas property that had seen better days. Unlike the glittering resorts that lined the Strip, the Golden Nugget was a relic from an earlier era, nestled in what was considered a declining part of the city. While many saw the property as a remnant of Las Vegas' past,

Wynn saw an opportunity to revitalize it and, in the process, breathe new life into the entire downtown area.

The acquisition of the Golden Nugget was a defining moment in Wynn's career. Using the skills he had honed in his early ventures, he set about transforming the once-faded property into a modern, upscale destination. Wynn's vision was revolutionary—he sought to combine the classic charm of old Las Vegas with a new level of sophistication and luxury. By upgrading the facilities, improving customer service, and introducing high-quality entertainment, Wynn turned the Golden Nugget into one of the most profitable casinos in the downtown area. His ability to recognize untapped potential became a hallmark of his career.

This revitalization of the Golden Nugget was more than just a business success—it signaled a shift in how casinos would operate. Wynn understood that customers wanted more than just a place to gamble; they sought an immersive experience, one that combined entertainment, luxury, and excitement. This realization would guide his future endeavors, as he expanded his influence and introduced the concept of the mega-resort, which would forever change the landscape of Las Vegas.

Wynn's success with the Golden Nugget allowed him to make a name for himself in the competitive casino world. As the property thrived, so did his reputation as an innovative businessman with a flair for turning around struggling operations. Wynn's approach to casino management, focused on enhancing the guest experience, earned him respect among his peers and paved the way for future expansions. His success downtown also provided him with the financial resources and confidence to set his sights on even bigger projects.

While the Golden Nugget laid the foundation for Wynn's career in the casino industry, it was only the beginning. His entry into the world of Las Vegas casinos was not marked by flashy purchases or immediate success; rather, it was the result of careful planning, strategic investments, and a deep understanding of both risk and opportunity. Wynn's ability to think beyond the traditional casino model, focusing on luxury, entertainment, and guest satisfaction, would become the driving force behind his later successes on the Strip.

Steve Wynn's early ventures into the casino world were characterized by his willingness to take risks, his attention to detail, and his belief that Las Vegas could become a destination for more than just gambling. As he moved from smaller investments to the ownership of major properties, Wynn continued to push the boundaries of what was possible in the casino industry. His entry into this world was the first step in a remarkable career that would see him transform Las Vegas into a global symbol of luxury and opulence.

Steve Wynn's entry into the casino world was driven by a combination of ambition, foresight, and his growing understanding of how to balance risk with opportunity. After his early success in the business world with his involvement in his father's bingo operations, Wynn recognized that the gambling industry held the potential for greater rewards and more expansive ventures. His eventual move into the Las Vegas casino scene would mark the start of his transformation into one of the most influential figures in the industry.

In the late 1960s, Las Vegas was already well-known as the go-to destination for entertainment and gambling, but the industry had yet to evolve into the luxurious, integrated experiences that it would later become. Wynn recognized this gap in the market. Rather than just focusing on gambling as a form of entertainment, he saw that customers could be drawn in by offering more: high-end dining, opulent accommodations, and world-class entertainment.

Initially, Wynn was an outsider in the world of casinos, but his investment in the Frontier Hotel helped him break into this exclusive circle. He spent time learning the ropes of the casino business, making important connections with key figures in the gaming world, and understanding the complexities of the industry from the inside. This early period gave him invaluable insights into how casinos were run, the logistics of managing such a large operation, and the financial strategies necessary to turn a profit in the highly competitive Las Vegas market.

The opportunity to make his mark came with the Golden Nugget, a historic property in downtown Las Vegas that had lost much of its luster. For many, the Golden Nugget represented the old Las Vegas, a relic of the city's earlier years that seemed out of place compared to the newer, flashier casinos on the Strip. But Wynn, with his keen business instincts, saw the property's untapped potential. He didn't just want to restore the Golden Nugget to its former glory; he wanted to transform it into something new, something that would set a standard for the casino industry.

Wynn's work at the Golden Nugget was revolutionary. He didn't simply renovate the building or update the gambling tables—he transformed the entire experience for his guests. He understood that people visiting Las Vegas wanted more than just to gamble; they wanted to be entertained and pampered, to feel as though they were part of something exclusive and extravagant. This was Wynn's guiding principle: he didn't just want to run a casino, he wanted to create a destination that offered a complete experience.

To achieve this, Wynn brought in high-end restaurants, glamorous entertainment acts, and luxurious hotel accommodations, all aimed at elevating the Golden Nugget's appeal. He carefully crafted the atmosphere, paying attention to details that would make his guests feel valued and indulged. Wynn's efforts turned the once-forgotten property into a thriving success and a symbol of the revitalization of downtown Las Vegas.

What set Wynn apart from many other casino operators at the time was his forward-thinking approach to the industry. He recognized that the future of gambling would lie in providing an all-encompassing experience for guests. People weren't just coming to casinos to gamble anymore; they were looking for luxury, entertainment, and relaxation. Wynn's ability to see this shift in the industry's direction is what made him so successful in the early stages of his career.

As Wynn's reputation grew, so did his influence in the world of casinos. His success with the Golden Nugget allowed him to expand his operations and explore new opportunities. He began to think bigger, envisioning casinos that would not only offer top-notch gambling but would also set a new standard for luxury resorts. This vision would eventually lead to the creation of some of the most iconic properties in Las Vegas, and beyond.

In addition to his business acumen, Wynn's personal style of leadership was also a major factor in his success. He was known for being deeply involved in every aspect of his properties, from the design of the casinos to the smallest details of guest service. He demanded excellence from his employees and expected that every guest who walked through his doors would receive the highest level of care and attention. This commitment to quality became one of the trademarks of a Wynn property.

The entry into the casino world was more than just a business venture for Wynn—it was the beginning of a legacy. He didn't simply want to run successful casinos; he wanted to change the way people thought about the casino experience. His ability to combine risk with innovation, his attention to detail, and his relentless pursuit of excellence all contributed to his rise as one of the most influential figures in the gaming industry. His early successes laid the foundation for what would become a transformative career, one that would redefine Las Vegas and set a new standard for luxury and entertainment worldwide.

CHAPTER 3: REINVENTING LAS VEGAS

Steve Wynn's reinvention of Las Vegas is one of the most remarkable achievements in modern business and urban development. When he arrived on the scene, Las Vegas was already a well-known destination for gambling, but it lacked the sophistication, glamour, and luxury that Wynn envisioned. What others saw as merely a city of neon lights, gambling halls, and quick entertainment, Wynn saw as a blank canvas, waiting to be transformed into a global center for opulence and experience. His vision went beyond simply building successful casinos—he wanted to change the very essence of the city and its reputation. Through his efforts, Las Vegas would evolve from a gambling town into a world-renowned luxury destination.

Wynn's first major step in reinventing Las Vegas began with the revitalization of the Golden Nugget in downtown. He saw the potential to bring a new level of elegance and sophistication to what was traditionally a rougher, more casual area of the city. Through a series of calculated improvements, Wynn turned the Golden Nugget into a symbol of luxury, blending the old-world charm of classic Las Vegas with modern amenities. This success, however, was just a prelude to his much larger ambitions.

Wynn's vision for transforming Las Vegas took full form with the construction of The Mirage, a groundbreaking resort that would revolutionize the casino industry. Opened in 1989, The Mirage was not just another casino—it was the first mega-resort, an entirely new concept that combined gambling, entertainment, and luxury under one roof. The Mirage was unlike anything Las Vegas had ever seen. It was designed to immerse guests in an exotic and enchanting environment, from its tropical-themed landscaping to the iconic volcano that erupted nightly in front of the resort. Wynn's goal was to create an experience where visitors could escape into a world of luxury and fantasy, and The Mirage delivered just that.

The development of The Mirage introduced a new level of scale and ambition to Las Vegas. It was the first resort to be built with over a billion-dollar budget, setting a precedent for what was possible in terms of both design and financial investment. The Mirage boasted lavish rooms, world-class entertainment, and a level of service that had rarely been seen in Las Vegas. It wasn't just a place to gamble—it was a full-fledged destination where guests could spend days enjoying the amenities without ever leaving the resort. This was a pivotal shift in how people thought about Las Vegas. No longer was it just a place for weekend gamblers; it was becoming a world-class destination where tourists from around the globe could come to experience luxury, entertainment, and indulgence.

The success of The Mirage set the stage for Wynn's next bold project: the Bellagio. Opened in 1998, the Bellagio represented the pinnacle of Wynn's vision for Las Vegas. Inspired by the Italian village of Bellagio on Lake Como, the resort was designed to exude elegance and sophistication at every turn. The Bellagio became known for its refined style, offering guests not only the chance to gamble but also access to world-class art, fine dining, and cultural experiences. One of the Bellagio's most iconic features was its massive, choreographed fountain show, set against a backdrop of the hotel's elegant facade. The fountains, like the erupting volcano at The Mirage, became a symbol of Wynn's flair for spectacle and innovation.

The Bellagio also helped to cement Las Vegas as a center for high-end entertainment. Wynn introduced Cirque du Soleil's "O," a permanent aquatic show that became one of the most successful and beloved productions in the city. The Bellagio's luxury also extended to its accommodations, with suites designed to rival the world's finest hotels, and its dining, which featured restaurants by renowned chefs. Wynn's insistence on incorporating fine art into the resort, including works from his own personal collection, further elevated the status of Las Vegas as more than just a gambling town—it was becoming a cultural hub as well.

Wynn's reinvention of Las Vegas didn't stop at individual resorts. He was instrumental in transforming the entire Las Vegas Strip into a new kind of destination, attracting visitors not just for the gaming tables, but for the luxury resorts, high-end shopping, fine dining, and world-class entertainment. His projects inspired other developers to follow suit, leading to a wave of mega-resorts that mirrored the grandeur and scale of The Mirage and Bellagio. The Strip, once dominated by smaller, themed casinos, was now lined with towering, luxurious resorts that catered to a new breed of traveler: one who expected more than just a quick gambling fix.

Wynn's ability to blend entertainment, luxury, and innovation changed the city's image. Las Vegas was no longer seen as just a place for gamblers and weekend revelers; it was a premier destination for the wealthy, the famous, and those seeking a unique blend of entertainment and indulgence. Wynn's influence extended far beyond Las Vegas, as the model of the mega-resort spread to other cities and regions around the world. He set a new standard for what a casino could be, one that emphasized luxury, creativity, and a complete guest experience.

Through Wynn's efforts, Las Vegas became a symbol of opulence, extravagance, and innovation. His reinvention of the city attracted not only tourists but also global investors, high-end brands, and some of the world's top entertainers. What once was a city focused primarily on gambling now offered something for everyone: from the casual traveler to the ultra-wealthy. Steve Wynn's vision and determination changed the face of Las Vegas, turning it into one of the world's most iconic destinations, and his legacy continues to shape the city's identity today.

Revitalizing Downtown: The Golden Nugget's Transformation

Steve Wynn's revitalization of downtown Las Vegas through the transformation of the Golden Nugget is often regarded as a turning point in both his career and in the evolution of Las Vegas itself. At a time when the glittering Las Vegas Strip was quickly becoming the centerpiece of the city's tourism industry, Wynn took a calculated gamble on a property that many viewed as a relic of the past. The Golden Nugget, located in the heart of downtown Las Vegas on Fremont Street, was one of the city's oldest casinos, but by the time Wynn acquired it, it had fallen into disrepair and was seen as outdated compared to the grander casinos that lined the Strip. However, Wynn's ability to see potential where others saw decay was crucial to his success. His transformation of the Golden Nugget not only revitalized the property but also breathed new life into the downtown area.

When Wynn took control of the Golden Nugget, he approached the project with a bold vision. He didn't just want to restore the property to its former glory; he wanted to create something entirely new, something that would combine the charm of old Las Vegas with the opulence and modernity that would define its future. Wynn's first priority was to upgrade the Golden

Nugget's physical infrastructure. The property was in need of extensive renovations, and Wynn spared no expense in making the necessary improvements. He updated the casino floor, upgraded the rooms, and gave the entire building a much-needed facelift. However, his ambitions went far beyond cosmetic changes. Wynn understood that the guest experience was key to revitalizing the Golden Nugget, and he set about creating an environment where luxury and entertainment were central to the casino's identity.

One of the key elements of Wynn's approach to transforming the Golden Nugget was his focus on customer service. He believed that the success of a casino was not just about offering games of chance but about offering an unparalleled level of service that would make guests feel special and valued. Under Wynn's leadership, the Golden Nugget became known for its exceptional hospitality, with a staff that was trained to cater to the needs of guests at every level. This emphasis on service helped set the Golden Nugget apart from other downtown casinos and created a new standard for how casinos should operate.

Wynn also brought a new level of sophistication to the property. Recognizing that Las Vegas was attracting more affluent tourists, he sought to appeal to a higher-end clientele by offering luxury accommodations, fine dining, and exclusive entertainment. Wynn's vision included the introduction of gourmet restaurants, where guests could enjoy world-class cuisine, a stark contrast to the inexpensive buffets that had traditionally defined Las Vegas dining. This elevated dining experience was a crucial part of Wynn's strategy to attract a more discerning audience and helped solidify the Golden Nugget's reputation as a premier destination in downtown Las Vegas.

Another significant aspect of Wynn's transformation of the Golden Nugget was his focus on entertainment. He understood that gambling was only one part of what Las Vegas had to offer and that guests were increasingly looking for more diverse forms of entertainment. To meet this demand, Wynn introduced high-quality entertainment acts to the Golden Nugget, including major headliners and performances that brought a sense of spectacle to the property. This blend of gambling, dining, and entertainment created a more holistic experience for guests and made the Golden Nugget a must-visit destination in downtown Las Vegas.

Wynn's efforts to modernize the Golden Nugget also included substantial investments in the property's physical space. He expanded the casino floor, added luxurious new suites, and redesigned the interior to reflect a more contemporary aesthetic while still retaining the charm that had made the Golden Nugget an iconic part of Las Vegas history. These changes were aimed at creating a space where guests could not only gamble but also relax and enjoy a lavish experience. The new look of the Golden Nugget was a reflection of Wynn's larger vision for the future of Las Vegas—a city where luxury, entertainment, and gambling were seamlessly integrated.

Wynn's revitalization of the Golden Nugget had a profound impact not only on the property itself but also on the broader downtown area. Before Wynn's intervention, downtown Las Vegas had been in decline, overshadowed by the rapid growth and glitzy new developments on the Strip. By transforming the Golden Nugget into a thriving, upscale destination, Wynn brought new attention to the downtown area and helped to spark a revitalization that would continue for years to come. The success of the Golden Nugget demonstrated that downtown Las Vegas could still be a viable and attractive part of the city's tourism landscape, and other developers soon followed suit, investing in the area and helping to restore its vitality.

Wynn's success with the Golden Nugget also had a significant impact on his career. The transformation of the property established him as one of the most innovative and visionary leaders in the casino industry. It was the first major project where he was able to fully implement his vision of creating a luxury casino experience, and its success laid the groundwork for his future ventures, including the groundbreaking development of The Mirage and the Bellagio. The Golden Nugget became a symbol of Wynn's ability to blend the old and the new, combining the history of Las Vegas with a modern, luxurious twist.

Through his work at the Golden Nugget, Wynn demonstrated that he had a unique ability to not only revitalize struggling properties but also to elevate the entire guest experience in a way that had never been seen before. The Golden Nugget became a model for future developments, where the focus was not just on gambling but on creating a holistic resort experience that included high-end accommodations, gourmet dining, entertainment, and unparalleled service. This approach would come to define Wynn's career and his impact on the Las Vegas landscape.

In revitalizing the Golden Nugget, Steve Wynn set the stage for his future successes and left an indelible mark on the city of Las Vegas. His transformation of the property breathed new life into downtown and proved that with vision, innovation, and a commitment to excellence, even a historic casino could be reimagined and made relevant again in the modern age. The Golden Nugget became a symbol of Wynn's larger vision for the future of Las Vegas—a place where luxury, entertainment, and history could coexist and thrive together.

The Mirage – The Game Changer

The opening of The Mirage in 1989 marked a turning point not only for Steve Wynn's career but also for the entire Las Vegas Strip. It is often regarded as the project that transformed the concept of a casino from merely a gambling hall into a comprehensive resort experience. Wynn had already made a name for himself with his successful revitalization of the Golden Nugget in downtown Las Vegas, but The Mirage was a different kind of undertaking, a grand and ambitious project that set a new standard for luxury, entertainment, and scale.

Wynn envisioned The Mirage not just as a casino but as a destination that would redefine what visitors expected from Las Vegas.

When Wynn conceived of The Mirage, Las Vegas was in a transitional phase. The city was moving away from its association with cheap gambling and kitschy entertainment, but it hadn't yet developed the world-class reputation that it enjoys today. Wynn's bold concept for The Mirage was to bridge that gap. It would be the first mega-resort on the Strip, and its success would serve as a template for the future of the industry.

One of the most significant aspects of The Mirage's construction was its sheer size and scope. It was the first resort in Las Vegas to be built with a budget exceeding a billion dollars, a level of financial investment that was unheard of at the time. Wynn wasn't interested in simply creating a bigger casino; he wanted to create a complete, immersive experience. This was reflected in every aspect of the resort's design, from its iconic golden windows to its lush landscaping, which included tropical plants, waterfalls, and lagoons. The Mirage was designed to transport visitors to a different world, one that was both luxurious and exotic.

At the heart of Wynn's vision for The Mirage was the idea of creating a spectacle. He understood that Las Vegas was a city built on entertainment and that in order to stand out, a casino had to offer something unique and memorable. One of the most famous examples of this is the Mirage's erupting volcano, which became a symbol of the resort and one of the most recognizable attractions on the Strip. The volcano, located at the front of the property, was a testament to Wynn's flair for drama and his understanding of the power of visual impact. Every night, crowds would gather to watch the volcano "erupt" in a choreographed display of fire, light, and water. It was more than just a clever marketing gimmick; it was part of Wynn's larger strategy to create an experience that extended beyond the gaming floor.

The Mirage was also groundbreaking in terms of its focus on luxury and guest experience. Wynn understood that the future of Las Vegas lay not just in attracting gamblers but in appealing to a wider audience of tourists, including families, couples, and international travelers. He introduced a range of upscale amenities that had never before been seen in Las Vegas. The resort featured elegant rooms and suites, designed with a level of attention to detail that was more commonly associated with high-end hotels in cities like New York or Paris. Wynn wanted every aspect of a guest's stay at The Mirage to feel indulgent, from the accommodations to the dining options and entertainment.

One of the most notable innovations that Wynn introduced at The Mirage was the concept of a casino-resort that offered more than just gambling. The Mirage was the first casino to successfully integrate luxury dining, world-class entertainment, and extravagant amenities into a single experience. Wynn brought in celebrity chefs to open high-end restaurants, a move that helped elevate Las Vegas's dining scene. He also introduced the concept of headliner entertainment, with shows that were designed to draw in guests who might not otherwise visit a casino. One of the most successful examples of this was Wynn's partnership with Cirque du Soleil, which debuted its aquatic-themed show "Mystère" at The Mirage. The show was an instant hit and helped establish Cirque du Soleil as a permanent fixture in Las Vegas, changing the landscape of live entertainment on the Strip.

In addition to its focus on luxury and entertainment, The Mirage was also innovative in terms of its business model. Wynn pioneered the use of Wall Street financing to fund the construction of the resort, a move that was considered risky at the time but ultimately proved to be a masterstroke. By securing large amounts of capital through bonds, Wynn was able to build The Mirage on a scale that was previously unimaginable. The success of The Mirage demonstrated that Las Vegas could support luxury mega-resorts, and it paved the way for future developments, including Wynn's later projects like the Bellagio.

The Mirage also helped to reshape the image of Las Vegas. Before its opening, the city was often seen as a somewhat seedy destination, known more for its cheap thrills and quick getaways than for its sophistication. The Mirage changed that perception. By offering a world-class experience that combined luxury, entertainment, and gaming, The Mirage helped transform Las Vegas into a global destination for tourists seeking indulgence, relaxation, and excitement. It attracted a new type of visitor—people who came not just to gamble but to experience the high-end amenities, the fine dining, and the top-tier shows that Wynn had built into the resort.

Moreover, The Mirage set the stage for a new era of competition on the Strip. Its success proved that there was a market for large-scale, luxury resorts, and it inspired other developers to follow Wynn's lead. In the years following its opening, several other mega-resorts were built, each one trying to outdo the last in terms of size, luxury, and spectacle. The Las Vegas Strip was transformed into a collection of extravagant resorts, each offering its own unique combination of gambling, entertainment, and luxury experiences. The Mirage was the catalyst for this transformation, and its influence can still be seen in the design and philosophy of modern Las Vegas resorts.

Wynn's ability to combine entertainment, luxury, and spectacle at The Mirage was nothing short of revolutionary. He understood that Las Vegas was a city built on fantasy, and he tapped into that by creating an experience that was both immersive and indulgent. The Mirage set a new standard for what a casino-resort could be, and its success helped to cement Wynn's reputation as one of the most visionary figures in the gaming and hospitality industries.

The transformation of Las Vegas, driven in large part by Steve Wynn's vision for The Mirage, is a story of reinvention and ambition. Wynn didn't just want to create a casino; he wanted to reshape the entire concept of what a Las Vegas resort could be. Before The Mirage, Las Vegas casinos primarily focused on gambling, with dining, accommodations, and entertainment as secondary features. Wynn shifted this focus, aiming to provide an all-encompassing luxury experience where every detail was meticulously crafted to impress guests.

Wynn's approach was built on the idea that Las Vegas needed more than just slot machines and poker tables to attract visitors in the long term. The Mirage would cater to an increasingly diverse audience, including high-rollers, families, and international tourists. The goal was to make Las Vegas not only a gambling haven but also a destination known for its high-end amenities, entertainment, and relaxation. This was a pioneering idea at the time, and Wynn's ability to execute it with flair forever changed the landscape of the Strip.

From the moment guests arrived at The Mirage, they were greeted with something entirely new and captivating. The lush tropical theme, inspired by the South Pacific, was unlike anything else on the Strip. Waterfalls, palm trees, and the famous erupting volcano created an atmosphere of escape and fantasy, setting a new standard for immersive environments in the casino industry. Wynn understood that spectacle was key to attracting and retaining guests, and this element became one of the Mirage's most iconic features.

Inside The Mirage, Wynn spared no expense in creating a luxurious experience. The casino floor was expansive, but it was only one aspect of the resort. High-end shops, gourmet dining options, and a massive pool area, complete with cabanas and waterfalls, gave guests a sense of luxury that had previously been reserved for the most elite hotels around the world. Wynn's attention to detail extended to every aspect of the guest experience, from the quality of the linens in the rooms to the level of personalized service provided by the staff.

Perhaps one of the most revolutionary aspects of The Mirage was Wynn's emphasis on entertainment. Rather than relying solely on gambling, The Mirage became a place where people came for world-class shows and performances. Wynn introduced a permanent Cirque du Soleil production, *Mystère*, which was unlike any other show on the Strip. This was the first time Las Vegas had seen a production of this scale, combining acrobatics, theater, and spectacle into a mesmerizing experience. Wynn understood that entertainment could be just as much of a draw as gambling, and *Mystère* became a cornerstone of The Mirage's appeal.

Wynn's insistence on offering top-tier dining was another aspect of The Mirage that set it apart. At a time when most Las Vegas casinos were known for their affordable buffets, The Mirage introduced fine dining on a grand scale. Wynn recruited world-renowned chefs to create unique dining experiences, offering guests a level of culinary excellence that was previously unheard of in Las Vegas. This move elevated the city's dining scene and helped redefine Las Vegas as a destination for foodies as well as gamblers.

Financially, The Mirage was a bold gamble in its own right. Wynn pioneered the use of Wall Street financing to build the resort, securing massive loans to fund the project. This was a risky move, as no other casino had been financed on such a large scale. Many industry insiders were skeptical that such a massive investment would pay off, but Wynn's vision proved to be a resounding success. The Mirage was an instant hit, with visitors flocking to experience the next level of luxury and entertainment that Wynn had created. Its financial success not only validated Wynn's approach but also encouraged other developers to pursue similarly ambitious projects.

The impact of The Mirage on Las Vegas was far-reaching. Its success helped usher in a new era of mega-resorts, where the focus was on creating an all-encompassing experience rather than just a gambling floor. Wynn had demonstrated that Las Vegas could attract a much broader audience by offering luxury, entertainment, and relaxation alongside gaming. This model became the blueprint for future resorts, including Wynn's later developments like The Bellagio, as well as other landmark properties such as The Venetian and The Wynn.

In the wake of The Mirage's success, Las Vegas underwent a period of rapid growth and transformation. The Strip saw an influx of investment as developers raced to create bigger and more elaborate resorts, each one trying to outdo the last in terms of luxury, spectacle, and entertainment. The Mirage set a precedent, not only for the scale of its offerings but also for the integration of non-gaming elements that could attract a wider variety of visitors. Las Vegas, once known primarily as a gambler's paradise, was now becoming a global entertainment capital.

Wynn's work on The Mirage fundamentally changed the way people viewed Las Vegas. The city was no longer just a place for cheap thrills and gambling. It was now a world-class destination, known for its luxury, sophistication, and world-renowned entertainment. The success of The Mirage solidified Wynn's reputation as one of the most innovative and influential figures in the casino and hospitality industries, and his vision for the future of Las Vegas became the new standard for the industry as a whole.

Through The Mirage, Steve Wynn demonstrated that Las Vegas could offer more than just gambling. It could be a city of luxury, where guests came to be entertained, pampered, and immersed in an experience that was as much about spectacle as it was about placing a bet. This shift in thinking set Las Vegas on a path of transformation that continues to this day, with Wynn's influence still visible in every corner of the Strip.

CHAPTER 4: BELLAGIO – THE PINNACLE OF LUXURY

Steve Wynn's creation of the Bellagio in 1998 is widely considered the pinnacle of luxury in Las Vegas, solidifying his reputation as a visionary in the world of hospitality and entertainment. The Bellagio was not just another resort and casino; it was a testament to Wynn's relentless pursuit of perfection and his commitment to elevating Las Vegas to a destination that would rival the world's most prestigious cities. With the Bellagio, Wynn aimed to set a new standard for what a luxury resort could be, pushing the boundaries of design, art, and opulence.

The inspiration for the Bellagio came from Wynn's love of European elegance, particularly the beauty and charm of Lake Como in northern Italy. He envisioned creating an environment that would capture the essence of Old World luxury, infused with the refinement and artistic sensibilities of European aristocracy. From its grand architecture to the smallest details in its design, the Bellagio was crafted to evoke the grandeur of an Italian palazzo, where guests could experience unparalleled elegance in every facet of their stay.

The centerpiece of the Bellagio was, and still remains, its iconic man-made lake, covering more than eight acres. This vast expanse of water, situated directly in front of the resort, was an integral part of Wynn's vision. The lake, with its stunning water fountains, became a signature feature, drawing millions of visitors who came to witness the choreographed fountain shows that would take place several times a day. The Bellagio fountains were not just a spectacle; they were a work of art. The water danced in sync with classical and contemporary music, creating an unforgettable experience for anyone who watched. The fountains, along with the lake, added an air of sophistication and tranquility to the hustle and bustle of the Las Vegas Strip, reinforcing the idea that the Bellagio was a retreat from the ordinary.

Beyond the lake and fountains, Wynn focused on the interior of the Bellagio, creating spaces that exuded luxury at every turn. The Bellagio lobby set the tone for what guests could expect, featuring the famous *Fiori di Como*, a breathtaking glass sculpture by renowned artist Dale Chihuly. Comprising over 2,000 hand-blown glass flowers, this ceiling installation was an example of the kind of artistry Wynn wanted to showcase at the Bellagio. His commitment to integrating fine art into the resort went beyond this single piece; the Bellagio was home to one of the first galleries in Las Vegas to display high-caliber art. The Bellagio Gallery of Fine Art featured works from the likes of Picasso, Monet, and Van Gogh, among others. Wynn believed that fine art should be accessible to the public, and he used the Bellagio as a platform to bring some of the world's greatest masterpieces to Las Vegas.

The Bellagio also broke new ground in its approach to dining. Wynn brought Michelin-starred chefs and world-renowned restaurateurs to the resort, transforming the way people thought about dining in Las Vegas. Before the Bellagio, the city's culinary scene was primarily focused on affordable buffets and casual eateries. Wynn aimed to change this by offering fine dining experiences that could compete with the best restaurants in cities like Paris, New York, and Tokyo. Restaurants like Le Cirque and Picasso became instant hits, attracting food connoisseurs from around the world. Wynn's insistence on culinary excellence helped Las Vegas gain recognition as a global dining destination, a status that endures to this day.

The casino floor at the Bellagio was also a departure from the typical Las Vegas experience. While most casinos were loud, bright, and crowded, Wynn designed the Bellagio's gaming areas to feel more refined and exclusive. The high-limit rooms, in particular, were designed to cater to the most discerning gamblers, offering a level of privacy and luxury that was unmatched at the time. Everything from the décor to the service was intended to make players feel like they were part of an elite, sophisticated world. The gaming experience at the Bellagio was not about volume or quantity; it was about quality and the creation of an environment where guests felt special.

Accommodations at the Bellagio were another area where Wynn's commitment to luxury was evident. The rooms and suites were designed with a level of attention to detail that was previously unheard of in Las Vegas. Wynn brought in the finest materials, from marble floors to custom furnishings, to ensure that every aspect of a guest's stay was luxurious. The suites, in particular, offered panoramic views of the lake and fountains, allowing guests to enjoy the beauty of the Bellagio's surroundings from the comfort of their rooms. Wynn understood that luxury was not just about opulence but also about comfort and service, and he made sure that the Bellagio excelled in all of these areas.

Entertainment at the Bellagio was equally groundbreaking. Wynn continued his successful partnership with Cirque du Soleil, commissioning the creation of *O*, a water-themed show that remains one of the most popular performances in Las Vegas. The theater for *O* was custom-built to accommodate a massive pool of water, where performers executed stunning aquatic acrobatics. The show was a perfect fit for the Bellagio, combining Wynn's love for spectacle with the resort's water theme. Like the Mirage before it, the Bellagio helped to elevate Las Vegas's entertainment scene, proving that the city could host world-class performances that attracted visitors for more than just gambling.

The Bellagio's overall design and layout were also carefully planned to create a sense of tranquility and escape. Wynn incorporated lush gardens, including the Bellagio Conservatory and Botanical Gardens, which featured seasonal displays of flowers and plants. This focus on nature and beauty further distinguished the Bellagio from its competitors, reinforcing the idea that guests were entering a luxurious retreat. The conservatory became a popular attraction in its own right, with visitors flocking to see the elaborate floral arrangements and installations.

Financially, the Bellagio was another enormous risk for Wynn, just as The Mirage had been nearly a decade earlier. The resort cost an unprecedented amount to build, and many doubted whether Las Vegas could support such a high-end property. However, Wynn's gamble paid off once again. The Bellagio became an immediate success, drawing high-profile guests from around the world and helping to further shift Las Vegas's reputation from a gambling-centric destination to a global hub of luxury and entertainment.

The Bellagio's influence on Las Vegas and the broader hospitality industry was profound. It set a new benchmark for luxury resorts, not just in Las Vegas but globally. The Bellagio proved that Las Vegas could compete with the finest hotels and resorts in the world, attracting a clientele that was interested in more than just gambling. The success of the Bellagio paved the way for the development of other high-end properties, both in Las Vegas and elsewhere, as developers sought to replicate Wynn's model of combining luxury, art, entertainment, and fine dining.

For Steve Wynn, the Bellagio was more than just a successful business venture. It was the realization of his lifelong dream to create the ultimate luxury resort. The Bellagio represented the culmination of all the lessons he had learned throughout his career, from his early days in the gaming industry to his success with The Mirage. It was a project that reflected his personal taste, his passion for art, and his belief that Las Vegas could be a city that offered the very best in luxury, entertainment, and hospitality. The Bellagio remains a testament to Wynn's vision, creativity, and relentless pursuit of excellence. The creation of the Bellagio marked a turning point in both Steve Wynn's career and the evolution of Las Vegas. Wynn had already redefined the city with The Mirage, but with the Bellagio, he took his vision to an entirely new level. The Bellagio was conceived as more than just a resort and casino—it was designed to be a symbol of luxury, artistry, and refined taste, challenging the perception of Las Vegas as a destination primarily for gamblers. Wynn's ambition for the Bellagio was clear from the start: he wanted to create the most luxurious and elegant resort in the world.

Inspired by the beauty and sophistication of the Italian region of Lake Como, the Bellagio aimed to capture the timeless elegance of European aristocratic estates. Wynn was deeply involved in every detail of the resort's design and construction, ensuring that the finished product would meet his exacting standards. From its grandiose architecture to the smallest decorative details, the Bellagio exuded an air of Old World charm, combined with the modern luxuries that Wynn believed would appeal to a discerning global clientele.

One of the most iconic features of the Bellagio was its sprawling man-made lake, which became an instant symbol of the resort. The eight-acre lake was not just a decorative element; it was a key part of Wynn's vision to create a serene and beautiful environment amidst the chaos of the Las Vegas Strip. The lake featured the now-famous Fountains of Bellagio, a choreographed water show that captivated audiences from the moment the resort opened. The fountains were carefully designed to synchronize with a selection of music, ranging from classical compositions to contemporary hits, creating an unforgettable visual and auditory experience. The sight of the water soaring into the sky in perfect harmony with the music became one of the most recognizable spectacles in Las Vegas, drawing visitors from all over the world.

Wynn's focus on art and culture was a defining feature of the Bellagio. The resort was the first in Las Vegas to house a fine art gallery, showcasing works from some of the world's most famous artists, including Pablo Picasso, Claude Monet, and Vincent van Gogh. Wynn's decision to integrate fine art into the fabric of the Bellagio was revolutionary. He believed that Las Vegas could be more than a hub for gambling and entertainment—it could also be a place where guests experienced high culture and sophistication. The Bellagio Gallery of Fine Art became a major draw for visitors who might not have otherwise considered a trip to Las Vegas, positioning the city as a destination for those seeking a more cultured experience.

Another groundbreaking element of the Bellagio was its approach to dining. Wynn recognized early on that the future of Las Vegas would depend on diversifying its appeal, and fine dining was one of the key ways to do so. He brought in world-renowned chefs and restaurateurs to create a culinary experience that would rival the best dining establishments in cities like Paris and New York. Restaurants such as Le Cirque and Picasso, which featured Michelin-starred chefs, became destinations in their own right, attracting food enthusiasts from across the globe. This emphasis on high-end cuisine was instrumental in transforming Las Vegas into a premier culinary destination, elevating the city's dining scene to new heights and setting a precedent that other resorts would soon follow.

The Bellagio's accommodations were equally luxurious, offering guests an experience that was unparalleled at the time. The rooms and suites were designed with impeccable attention to detail, featuring high-end finishes and custom furnishings that reflected Wynn's commitment to creating a refined and elegant atmosphere. Wynn believed that luxury was about more than just opulence; it was about providing guests with comfort and service that exceeded their expectations. The suites, with their panoramic views of the lake and fountains, were particularly coveted, offering a sense of exclusivity and privacy that was unmatched in Las Vegas.

Wynn's emphasis on entertainment at the Bellagio was another area where he broke new ground. Building on the success of his partnership with Cirque du Soleil at The Mirage, Wynn commissioned a new Cirque show, *O*, specifically for the Bellagio. The water-themed production, set in a custom-built theater with a massive pool of water, became one of the most popular shows in Las Vegas. *O* was a perfect fit for the Bellagio, combining Wynn's love of spectacle with the resort's water-centric theme. The show's combination of acrobatics, theater, and aquatic elements created a mesmerizing experience that further cemented the Bellagio as a destination for world-class entertainment. Wynn's foresight in integrating high-caliber performances into the Bellagio's offerings helped elevate Las Vegas's status as a global entertainment capital.

In addition to its art, dining, and entertainment, the Bellagio was renowned for its gardens and outdoor spaces. Wynn incorporated lush landscapes throughout the property, most notably in the Bellagio Conservatory and Botanical Gardens. These gardens, which featured rotating seasonal displays of flowers, plants, and trees, became one of the resort's most popular attractions. Wynn understood the importance of creating an environment where guests could escape the intensity of the casino and the Strip, and the conservatory provided a peaceful, beautiful retreat that reinforced the Bellagio's reputation as a luxurious oasis.

The Bellagio's casino was also designed with Wynn's signature attention to detail. Unlike the loud, flashy casinos typical of Las Vegas, the Bellagio's gaming floor was elegant and refined, with an emphasis on comfort and service. Wynn created high-limit rooms for the most exclusive guests, offering a level of privacy and luxury that had never been seen in the city's casinos. The Bellagio's casino was not about volume or flash; it was about creating a sophisticated gaming experience for those seeking a more refined environment.

The success of the Bellagio proved once again that Steve Wynn's vision for Las Vegas was ahead of its time. The resort's combination of luxury, art, dining, and entertainment attracted a diverse and upscale clientele, setting a new standard for what a Las Vegas resort could be. Financially, the Bellagio was a massive success, generating unprecedented revenues and encouraging other developers to follow Wynn's lead in creating high-end, all-encompassing resorts. Wynn had not only redefined luxury in Las Vegas; he had reshaped the city's identity as a world-class destination for more than just gambling.

The Bellagio remains one of the most iconic and successful resorts in Las Vegas to this day, a testament to Steve Wynn's vision and ambition. It represents the culmination of his career-long pursuit of excellence and his belief that Las Vegas could become a city of sophistication, culture, and refinement. Through the Bellagio, Wynn created a legacy of luxury that continues to influence the hospitality and entertainment industries, both in Las Vegas and beyond.

Redefining Casino Culture: High-End Elegance in Las Vegas

Steve Wynn's approach to redefining casino culture, particularly through the lens of high-end elegance in Las Vegas, was revolutionary. Before his influence, Las Vegas was synonymous with flashy neon lights, budget-friendly buffets, and an entertainment scene primarily focused on gambling. Wynn, however, had a different vision. He sought to transform the city's image, moving it from a kitschy, gambler-driven destination to a world-class luxury haven that could attract high-end tourists, business executives, and even art lovers. His projects, including The Mirage, Bellagio, and later Wynn Las Vegas, embodied this shift, with a focus on refined elegance, exclusivity, and cultural sophistication.

Wynn's first significant foray into reshaping casino culture came with The Mirage, a property that set the stage for a new standard in Las Vegas. Rather than creating just another place to gamble, Wynn made The Mirage into a full-fledged resort experience. This marked a key turning point in Las Vegas's history, as Wynn introduced the concept of a mega-resort that was as much about luxury and leisure as it was about gambling. Guests were no longer just players on the casino floor but were treated as VIPs who expected luxury in every aspect of their stay—from dining to entertainment to relaxation.

The Mirage's success demonstrated that the gambling public was evolving. People were willing to spend more for an experience that offered elegance and exclusivity. Wynn understood that the modern guest was not simply looking for a place to play blackjack or roll dice. They wanted an entire ecosystem of luxury amenities, from high-end restaurants and sophisticated entertainment options to exquisite rooms and lavish surroundings. Wynn tapped into this desire by transforming Las Vegas into a city that could rival other luxury vacation destinations like Monte Carlo or the French Riviera.

The most dramatic demonstration of Wynn's commitment to high-end elegance came with the Bellagio. From the outset, the Bellagio was designed to be an opulent, European-inspired luxury resort, far from the rowdy, neon-drenched casinos of old Las Vegas. Wynn's goal was to elevate the gaming experience to one of class and refinement, transforming the traditional image of casinos as bustling, chaotic places into a sanctuary of calm sophistication. The Bellagio's atmosphere was subdued, with soft lighting, elegant furnishings, and an architectural style that borrowed heavily from the grandeur of Italian palaces. This was Wynn's answer to the changing tastes of guests—he gave them luxury in every detail, both in and out of the casino.

The gaming floor at the Bellagio was a major departure from the norm. While most casinos were loud and designed to keep gamblers playing for as long as possible through an assault of bright lights and constant noise, Wynn focused on creating an environment where elegance and high-stakes gaming could coexist. The Bellagio's casino exuded exclusivity and restraint, a place where discerning guests could enjoy their favorite games without the garish distractions typically associated with Vegas. Wynn made it clear that gaming at his properties was an experience in itself, where high-end design and exceptional service were just as important as the games being played.

One of the Bellagio's most striking features was the high-limit gaming salons, which Wynn designed for an elite clientele. These rooms were worlds away from the main casino floor, offering privacy, luxury, and personal service that was previously unheard of in Las Vegas. High rollers were treated not as faceless gamblers but as VIP guests, with access to the finest amenities, from personal butlers to private dining. These high-limit rooms signified Wynn's commitment to creating an environment where luxury was synonymous with gambling. He recognized that the future of Las Vegas lay not in catering to the masses but in appealing to a smaller, more exclusive clientele who would pay a premium for elegance and privacy.

In addition to the gaming experience, Wynn's emphasis on high-end dining and entertainment further redefined casino culture. Before his influence, dining in Las Vegas was largely an afterthought, dominated by buffets and casual eateries meant to lure gamblers back to the casino as quickly as possible. Wynn, however, understood that the modern luxury guest was looking for more than just food—they wanted a dining experience. By bringing in Michelin-starred chefs and world-class restaurateurs, Wynn transformed Las Vegas into a global culinary destination. The restaurants at Bellagio, including Le Cirque and Picasso, offered gourmet experiences that were on par with the finest dining establishments in New York, Paris, or Tokyo. This focus on fine dining not only elevated Las Vegas's reputation but also attracted a different kind of guest—those who came not just to gamble but to enjoy an all-encompassing luxury experience.

Wynn's redefinition of casino culture extended beyond the casino floor and restaurants to encompass the entire resort experience. He believed that luxury was not confined to one area but should permeate every aspect of a guest's stay. At properties like the Bellagio and later Wynn Las Vegas, the design, landscaping, and amenities were all carefully curated to create a sense of opulence and exclusivity. From the grand architecture of the hotels to the lush, manicured gardens and the integration of fine art throughout the properties, every detail was designed to enhance the guest's experience of luxury. The Bellagio's Conservatory and Botanical Gardens, with their rotating seasonal displays, were just one example of how Wynn created a sense of beauty and calm in the midst of the bustling Las Vegas Strip. These features were not just decorative; they were part of Wynn's larger vision to transform Las Vegas into a destination that could compete with the world's best resorts.

Perhaps the most innovative aspect of Wynn's approach was his integration of fine art into the Bellagio and Wynn Las Vegas. By showcasing works from renowned artists like Picasso and Monet, Wynn blurred the line between a casino and an art gallery, once again elevating the cultural cachet of Las Vegas. His art collection became a central feature of his properties, giving guests access to masterpieces that they might otherwise have to travel to New York or Europe to see. This move was not just about aesthetics; it was part of Wynn's larger strategy to attract a more sophisticated, cultured clientele who valued art and refinement as much as they did gambling and entertainment.

The entertainment at Wynn's resorts also reflected his desire to create an experience of elegance. His collaboration with Cirque du Soleil, which began with *Mystère* at Treasure Island and continued with *O* at the Bellagio, brought world-class theater to Las Vegas. These shows combined acrobatics, music, and theater in a way that appealed to a more discerning audience. Rather than the traditional cabaret shows or lounge acts that had dominated Las Vegas entertainment for decades, Wynn offered sophisticated productions that became global attractions in their own right. *O*, with its water-themed acrobatics and stunning visuals, was perfectly in line with Wynn's vision for the Bellagio—an immersive experience of elegance and artistry that went far beyond the casino floor.

Steve Wynn's vision redefined casino culture, not just in Las Vegas but across the world. His focus on high-end elegance, exclusivity, and refined experiences paved the way for the modern luxury resort. By elevating the gaming experience to one of sophistication and cultural enrichment, Wynn attracted a new kind of guest to Las Vegas, one who valued luxury in all its forms. Through his emphasis on art, dining, entertainment, and design, Wynn forever changed the landscape of the city, transforming it into a global destination for those seeking the best the world has to offer. His legacy as the man who redefined casino culture continues to influence the industry, with his innovations setting the standard for luxury resorts worldwide.

CHAPTER 5: WYNN LAS VEGAS – A LEGACY BUILT IN GOLD

Wynn Las Vegas represents the culmination of Steve Wynn's decades-long career and is often regarded as his crowning achievement. It stands as a monument to his vision of Las Vegas as more than just a gambling hub—a destination for luxury, sophistication, and world-class experiences. Wynn Las Vegas was designed not just to be a casino, but a lifestyle resort, embodying the philosophy of high-end elegance that Wynn had introduced with his earlier properties like The Mirage and Bellagio. However, this time, Wynn set out to surpass all his previous accomplishments and solidify his legacy with a property that would redefine the concept of luxury in the global hospitality industry.

From the beginning, Wynn's ambition for Wynn Las Vegas was to create a resort that could compete on an international scale with the world's most luxurious hotels. This was not just about size or grandeur but about offering an experience of unrivaled quality and exclusivity. Located on the site of the old Desert Inn, Wynn Las Vegas was built from the ground up, a sprawling property that symbolized the epitome of opulence. The resort opened in 2005 and immediately set a new standard for what luxury could look like in Las Vegas.

One of the defining features of Wynn Las Vegas is its architecture. Unlike the typical flashy, neon-clad structures of the Las Vegas Strip, Wynn opted for a sleek, modern aesthetic that stood out for its simplicity and elegance. The bronze-tinted glass tower was designed to reflect the sun during the day and offer a warm, inviting glow at night. The curved, understated shape of the building was a departure from the more ostentatious designs found elsewhere on the Strip, signaling that Wynn Las Vegas was not just another resort, but a refined sanctuary for the discerning traveler.

The interior of Wynn Las Vegas was where Steve Wynn's vision for luxury truly came to life. Every aspect of the resort was meticulously designed to create an atmosphere of sophistication and comfort. From the lush landscaping surrounding the property to the high-end finishes in the guest rooms, no detail was too small for Wynn's attention. The guest accommodations were some of the most luxurious in Las Vegas at the time, with rooms that featured custom furnishings, floor-to-ceiling windows offering stunning views of the Strip or the resort's private golf course, and state-of-the-art technology. The design of the rooms was minimalist yet opulent, focusing on comfort and elegance rather than flashy decor.

Wynn's emphasis on art was once again a central element of Wynn Las Vegas. In fact, he incorporated his extensive personal art collection into the resort, showcasing masterpieces from renowned artists like

Picasso, Rembrandt, and Andy Warhol throughout the property. This move not only elevated the aesthetic of the resort but also reinforced Wynn's long-standing belief that Las Vegas could be a place of high culture, where guests could enjoy world-class art as part of their stay. The inclusion of fine art set Wynn Las Vegas apart from other resorts, attracting a clientele that appreciated the intersection of art, luxury, and entertainment.

In terms of dining, Wynn Las Vegas raised the bar even higher than its predecessors. Wynn curated an exceptional lineup of restaurants, partnering with some of the world's most renowned chefs to create a dining experience that was second to none. Guests could enjoy a variety of cuisines, from high-end steakhouses to contemporary Asian fusion, all while dining in beautifully designed spaces that reflected the elegance of the resort. The emphasis on fine dining continued Wynn's tradition of making Las Vegas a global culinary destination, with each restaurant offering an experience that rivaled the best eateries in cities like Paris and New York.

Entertainment was another area where Wynn Las Vegas set a new standard. Building on his successful partnership with Cirque du Soleil at The Mirage and Bellagio, Wynn commissioned a new show for his latest resort. *Le Rêve*, which was performed in a custom-built theater, became one of the most popular shows in Las Vegas. Like *O* at Bellagio, *Le Rêve* featured water-based performances, with a combination of acrobatics, dance, and theater. The production was not just a spectacle but an immersive experience, perfectly in line with Wynn's vision of offering guests something extraordinary at every turn. The theater itself was designed with innovation in mind, featuring an intimate, circular seating arrangement that gave every guest a perfect view of the stage.

Wynn Las Vegas also featured one of the most exclusive gaming environments in Las Vegas. The casino floor was elegant and subdued, with an emphasis on comfort and service. High-limit gaming rooms were available for elite guests, offering privacy and luxury that few other properties could match. Wynn understood that high rollers were not just looking for a place to gamble—they wanted a refined experience where every detail catered to their desires. This focus on the luxury gaming experience helped Wynn Las Vegas attract some of the wealthiest and most discerning gamblers from around the world.

In addition to the casino, Wynn Las Vegas offered a wide range of amenities that further reinforced its status as a world-class resort. The Wynn Golf Club, designed by Tom Fazio and Steve Wynn himself, was a major draw for guests seeking a more leisurely activity. The lush, beautifully landscaped course was the only golf course on the Strip at the time, offering players a serene escape from the hustle and bustle of Las Vegas. The Wynn Spa, with its luxurious treatments and serene environment, was another key feature, providing guests with a sanctuary of relaxation and wellness.

The retail experience at Wynn Las Vegas was also a key component of the resort's appeal. Wynn curated a collection of high-end boutiques featuring luxury brands such as Chanel, Louis Vuitton, and Cartier, allowing guests to indulge in world-class shopping without ever leaving the resort. This focus on luxury retail was part of Wynn's larger vision of creating a resort that offered everything a guest could desire, from dining and entertainment to relaxation and shopping, all within a single, elegant environment.

Wynn Las Vegas was more than just a resort; it was a lifestyle destination that reflected Steve Wynn's understanding of luxury and his belief in the importance of creating an all-encompassing experience. The property became a model for other resorts around the world, with its emphasis on quality, exclusivity, and guest service influencing the future of the global hospitality industry. Wynn's commitment to excellence in every aspect of the resort, from design and art to dining and entertainment, solidified his reputation as a visionary in the world of luxury resorts.

Wynn Las Vegas also marked the beginning of a new chapter in Steve Wynn's career. The success of the resort paved the way for its sister property, Encore, which opened in 2008 and further expanded the Wynn brand's influence in the luxury market. Together, Wynn Las Vegas and Encore became symbols of what Las Vegas could be—a city that offered the finest in luxury, sophistication, and entertainment, all in one place.

Ultimately, Wynn Las Vegas stands as a testament to Steve Wynn's legacy. It represents the culmination of his life's work, an embodiment of his belief that Las Vegas could be more than a gambler's paradise—it could be a destination for the world's most discerning travelers. The resort continues to be one of the most iconic and successful properties on the Las Vegas Strip, a shining example of Wynn's ability to turn a bold vision into reality. Through Wynn Las Vegas, Steve Wynn not only redefined luxury in Las Vegas but also left an indelible mark on the global hospitality industry, cementing his legacy as one of the most influential figures in the world of resorts and entertainment.

Wynn's International Expansion

Steve Wynn's ambitions were never confined to the boundaries of Las Vegas. After transforming the Strip with iconic properties like The Mirage, Bellagio, and Wynn Las Vegas, he turned his attention to the international stage, aiming to redefine luxury gaming and resort experiences beyond the United States. Wynn's international expansion began to materialize as he sought to tap into emerging global markets, particularly in Asia, where gaming was gaining momentum and luxury tourism was on the rise. His foray into the international arena not only expanded the Wynn Resorts brand but also elevated the global perception of what a luxury casino resort could be.

The centerpiece of Wynn's international expansion was Macau, the only place in China where gambling is legal. Macau had long been a gambling hub, but by the time

Wynn entered the scene, it was ready for a transformation similar to what he had achieved in Las Vegas. The Chinese government had opened Macau to foreign investment in the early 2000s, and this presented a golden opportunity for Wynn to replicate his success on a global scale. Wynn saw Macau not just as a lucrative market but as a canvas where he could build something even more extraordinary.

Wynn Macau opened its doors and was an instant success. The resort stood out for its signature focus on high-end luxury, attention to detail, and world-class service. While many of Macau's existing casinos were built to cater primarily to gamblers, Wynn introduced the same full-scale resort model he had pioneered in Las Vegas. The resort featured opulent accommodations, high-end dining options, lavish retail spaces, and top-tier entertainment, all set in an elegant, refined atmosphere that was designed to attract both the burgeoning middle class of China and high-rolling international travelers.

The design of Wynn Macau was a testament to Steve Wynn's commitment to blending luxury with local cultural elements. The resort's architecture was sleek and modern, but it also incorporated traditional Chinese design elements, creating a unique fusion that appealed to the tastes and preferences of Asian clientele. From its grand entrance to its serene gardens, every aspect of the resort was meticulously planned to offer guests an experience that was both luxurious and respectful of local culture. This attention to cultural nuance was key to Wynn's success in Macau, as it demonstrated his understanding of the market and his ability to adapt his brand to different global contexts.

Like his properties in Las Vegas, Wynn Macau was also home to an impressive art collection, further elevating its status as a luxury destination. The inclusion of fine art in the resort's public spaces helped differentiate Wynn Macau from its competitors, offering guests a sophisticated, cultural experience that went beyond gambling. This commitment to creating an environment of elegance and refinement helped Wynn attract a new demographic of visitors to Macau—tourists who were not just interested in gaming, but in the total luxury experience.

Wynn Macau also redefined the gaming experience in Asia. Wynn introduced exclusive, high-limit gaming salons, where privacy, discretion, and luxury were paramount. These high-roller rooms catered to the wealthiest players in the world, offering unparalleled service and personalized attention. Wynn understood that in the Asian market, particularly in China, there was a strong demand for privacy and exclusivity among high-net-worth individuals, and his resorts delivered on that expectation. By creating a gaming environment that combined sophistication with top-tier service, Wynn further solidified his reputation as a visionary in the global luxury casino industry.

Building on the success of Wynn Macau, Steve Wynn took his international expansion to the next level with the development of Wynn Palace, located on Macau's Cotai Strip. The Cotai Strip was an emerging area that many compared to the Las Vegas Strip, and it quickly became the epicenter of Macau's gaming and entertainment industry. Wynn Palace was designed to be even more opulent than Wynn Macau, showcasing Wynn's belief that each new project should surpass the last in terms of luxury, scale, and innovation.

Wynn Palace was nothing short of spectacular. The resort was designed around the theme of flowers, with elaborate floral displays and a lake featuring gondolas shaped like mythical creatures, creating a sense of fantasy and elegance. True to form, Wynn Palace blended Western luxury with Eastern cultural elements, from its design to its dining options. The resort featured lavish accommodations, state-of-the-art gaming facilities, and a collection of fine art that included works from both Western and Asian artists. Once again, Wynn had managed to create a destination that appealed not just to gamblers but to luxury travelers seeking an all-encompassing resort experience.

Wynn's expansion into Asia also played a key role in the global gaming industry's broader shift toward the region. As China's middle class grew and disposable income increased, Macau became a hub for high-end tourism, attracting visitors from across Asia and the world. Wynn was at the forefront of this transformation, helping to establish Macau as the world's leading gaming destination, overtaking Las Vegas in terms of gaming revenue. Wynn's ability to anticipate the market's potential and his commitment to delivering luxury experiences allowed him to capitalize on the region's economic growth, further cementing his legacy as a global leader in the casino and resort industry.

Beyond Macau, Wynn's international ambitions extended to other markets as well. He explored opportunities in countries like Japan, where the government was considering legalizing casino gaming. Although Japan has been slower to open up its market compared to Macau, Wynn was an early advocate of expanding the brand into Japan, recognizing the country's potential as a lucrative market for luxury gaming resorts. Wynn's interest in Japan demonstrated his foresight and ability to identify emerging opportunities in new regions, even as competition in the global casino industry intensified.

Steve Wynn's international expansion was about more than just building casinos—it was about exporting a philosophy of luxury and transforming global perceptions of what a gaming resort could be. His ventures in Macau not only elevated the Wynn Resorts brand to new heights but also set a new standard for luxury gaming in Asia. By focusing on elegance, exclusivity, and cultural sophistication, Wynn was able to create a unique offering that appealed to the world's wealthiest travelers, while also fostering economic growth and development in the regions where his resorts were located.

Ultimately, Wynn's international expansion solidified his place as a pioneer in the global luxury resort industry. His projects in Macau, particularly Wynn Macau and Wynn Palace, became models for other developers seeking to tap into the lucrative Asian market. His influence extended far beyond Las Vegas, shaping the future of gaming and luxury tourism on a global scale. Today, Wynn's international properties stand as a testament to his vision, ambition, and relentless pursuit of excellence, marking him as a transformative figure in both the gaming industry and the broader world of luxury hospitality.

CONCLUSION

Steve Wynn's legacy is not merely etched in the grandeur of the resorts he built but in the transformation of an entire industry. His name has become synonymous with luxury, innovation, and high-stakes creativity—qualities that have redefined what it means to experience hospitality on the grandest scale. Through his visionary leadership, Wynn reinvented the Las Vegas skyline, setting new standards for the global entertainment and resort industry.

Master of Opulence – Betting Big charts Wynn's journey from the uncertainties of his early life to his status as a pioneer of experiential luxury. His willingness to take risks—whether introducing the first mega-resort with The Mirage or incorporating fine art into his properties—reshaped how the world views casino resorts, pushing the boundaries of possibility in the hospitality world. Wynn's brilliance lay not only in his financial acumen but in his understanding that people were seeking more than just a place to stay—they wanted an unforgettable experience.

But Wynn's legacy is also marked by controversy and personal challenges that threatened to overshadow his accomplishments. His rise, as much as his fall, is a reminder of the complexities of power, influence, and ambition. Yet, even amid these struggles, his impact on the world of luxury hospitality is undeniable.

As the world looks toward the future of travel and luxury, Steve Wynn's influence remains profound. His resorts continue to set benchmarks for excellence, and his approach to integrating art, architecture, and entertainment into immersive experiences has been adopted globally. Wynn proved that opulence could be more than just material wealth; it could be a fully crafted experience where every detail mattered, from the texture of the carpets to the lights on the casino floor.

In the end, Wynn's story is one of betting big—not just financially, but creatively and personally. He gambled on ideas that others thought too risky and, in doing so, changed the face of modern hospitality. His legacy, though complex, will forever be linked with the evolution of Las Vegas into a world capital of luxury. Wynn's name will remain a symbol of grandeur, ambition, and the relentless pursuit of perfection, long after the neon lights fade.

www.ingramcontent.com/pod-product-compliance
Lightning Source LLC
Chambersburg PA
CBHW070347230526
45471CB00006B/2448